Words
about
God

to help you
worship Him

by Nicholas Choy

for Tehila

10 9 8 7 6 5 4 3 2 1
© Copyright 2012 Nicholas Choy
ISBN: 978-1-84550-778-7

Published by Christian Focus Publications
Geanies House, Fearn, Ross-shire,
IV20 1TW, Scotland, UK

www.christianfocus.com
email: *info@christianfocus.com*

Written and Illustrated
by Nicholas Choy
Printed in China

Dear Reader,

A valuable way of getting to know God is to look closely at what He has said and done throughout the Bible. In the many ways that He has spoken – in His laws, acts, proverbs, prophecies, and promises – His special personality is revealed to us. What follows are words that describe God based on this revelation, including not just the warm and delightful parts, but also the awe-inspiring and fearful aspects that appear throughout Scripture and life. Some words may be surprising, and others familiar, but they help paint a bigger picture of who God is, leading to a deeper sense of His glory.

It is my hope that this little book will encourage fuller worship of God in your home. For younger children, the basic idea behind each word is summarized in a short rhyme. For older children and adults, a more detailed paragraph follows. I have arranged the words according to the general order in which God's characteristics are introduced in the Bible. Most importantly, the biblical references for each word are listed at the bottom, so that your family can go directly to the source for further study.

May the conversations in our households be a fragrant offering to our Lord.

NC

Deuteronomy 6:4-9

Creator

God made everything –
sky, tree, and bird,
Even the little bug –
simply by His word.

When you make a drawing, you start with an empty piece of paper. In the same way, the world was empty before God made it. However, God didn't need to use pencils or paint to create the world; He simply spoke out His will and things appeared.

God's creation is special, because no one else can do it. On your next picnic, think twice before squashing that little bug, because you couldn't make a bug even if you wanted to. And if that small little animal that God made is so amazing, think of how miraculous a creature you are, and how powerful our **Creator** God is!

Genesis 1, Job 38, Psalm 104, Hebrews 11:3
see also **Incarnate, Nurturing**

Aseity

Ants are not elephants,
   and nights are not days.
But God differs from us
   in even more ways!

An ant cannot act or think like an elephant. Neither can we act or think like God because God is so different from us. **Aseity** is the independence of God from the things He created. In our short lives, our small bodies, and our simple thoughts, we are completely different from God. We can get to know God only because He decided to come to us through His Son, the God-man Jesus Christ.

Genesis 1:1, Exodus 33:20, Isaiah 55:8-9, John 1:1-3
*see also **Eternal, Holy, Incarnate, Revelation***

Spirit

Spirit, Counselor, Comforter and Friend,
You will be with the church —
time without end.

God continues to do things in the world today through His **Spirit**. Though you may not see the wind itself, you can see the many things it moves, like the waves of the ocean or the sails of a boat. However, unlike the wind, the Holy Spirit is more than an invisible force. He is one of the three persons of the Godhead. He is the Helper promised by Jesus before His return to heaven, and the guarantee of God's presence in the Church until Jesus' return.

Genesis 1:2, Acts 1:8, 1 Corinthians 3:16
*see also **Gracious, Nurturing, Trinity***

Word

Creation speaks loudly, let it be heard!
It declares God's glory,
and the might of His word.

Words are powerful. When your parents tell you to clean your room or brush your teeth, you know what they want through their words. In a much greater way, God's power is also revealed when He speaks. With words, God created the earth, the sky, the sea, and every living thing within it. With words, Jesus calmed the storm, cast out evil spirits, and raised the dead. And with words, the Holy Spirit continues to tell the good news of Jesus through the church. Because God expresses His will through words, Jesus is "the Word" because Jesus' life reveals His Father's wishes perfectly.

Genesis 1, John 1, Isaiah 55:11
*see also **Creator, Revelation***

Personal

God is a person,
not a force or a state,
Through His Son Jesus
we befriend and relate.

You can't really become friends with a rock or a cloud. If you told them a joke they wouldn't be able to laugh, because they are not alive. You also can't really become friends with a shrub or a flower. If you tried to play sports with them, it would not be very interesting because they cannot think or act.

You can only have a friendship with a being who is personal: someone who remembers, who thinks, and who acts. Our God is a **personal** God, because He does remember, He does think, He does act. In fact, human beings are personal because we are made in His image and have been given this quality by Him.

Genesis 4:26, Exodus 3:1-15, Isaiah 43:1-13
see also **Understanding, YHWH**

YHWH

These four strange letters are not part of some game. They are a great gift to us, God's own special name!

In the past, people were often given names that described them: Alexander the Great, Pepin the Short, Charles the Bald. The Bible is also full of names that describe God: Elohim means "strong, powerful and mighty God", El Shaddai means "nourishing, ever-present God", and El Elyon means "God who is the highest one". However, the most significant name of God is one that He personally shared with His people: **YHWH**. This is His covenantal name, the name which He uses in His special relationship with Israel. The Hebrew people considered this name so holy that they never wrote it down fully, leaving out the vowels, and its full pronunciation remains a mystery. Like the name that you would use in a declaration of love, such as a marriage certificate or a public engraving, God's covenantal name reveals the deep and powerful bond between Himself and His people.

Genesis 15, Exodus 3:15
*see also **Personal, One, Revelation***

Gracious

Family, friends, health, and love,
All gifts come from God above.

Our God is a **gracious** God: He is a rich God who gives many gifts. Imagine we had to pay for all the blessings listed above. How much would they cost? All are priceless gifts that we could never buy for ourselves. On top of this, God offers the most precious gift of all, eternal life with Him, paid for through the death of His Son, Jesus Christ.

Exodus 34:6, Psalm 145, Romans 5:15-21, Ephesians 2:1-10
*see also **Benevolent, Lamb***

Holy

God is so holy no one can come near, Except through Christ's blood, and in reverent fear.

The sun is a very hot place, so hot that we can't live on it. We have to stay far away, so that its heat does not burn us up. In fact, we cannot even stare at the sun, because its brightness can blind us. In the same way, God's **holiness** is like the sun's heat. He is so pure, powerful, and different that if He did not hide His glory, we would die in His presence. Many of the people in the Old Testament were afraid to see God because of this.

The only way that we can approach God is through the protection of Jesus: when He died on the cross, He traded with us His holiness for our sinfulness. Only with His holiness covering us can we have the courage to come near to God.

Exodus 19, Isaiah 6, Hebrews 10:19-23, Revelation 4
see also **Aseity, Eternal**

Deliverer

A bright and speeding ambulance
may rescue the very ill,
But only God brings sinners back
to life, through His holy will.

Exodus 15:1-21, Psalm 18, Psalm 70, Romans 11:26
see also **Just, King**

God brings people from one place to another. Through Moses, He delivered the Israelites from slavery in Egypt to a new home in Canaan. Through Jesus, He delivers His people from slavery in sin to freedom in life. An ambulance rushes a very sick person to be healed at the hospital, but our God is greater: He **delivers** us from a place of death to a place of eternal life.

Nurturing

As grapes only grow on the vine, So we need Christ, our lifeline.

In addition to creating life, God continues to **nurture** it. If He withdrew His breath, all of creation would grow dark and cold, like a city without power. And in addition to delivering us from sin, God continues to feed us spiritually. If He withdrew His Spirit, the church would wither away. Jesus calls Himself the True Vine because through him, God gives life to His people. Only through spiritual food such as worship, prayer and communion can we bear fruit for God's kingdom.

Job 38 & 39, Psalm 104, John 15
*see also **Creator, Deliverer, Faithful***

Benevolent

God is good, not only to me, But to the whole earth, to everybody.

God is good. He is not mean, He is not moody. He is good not only to those who love Him, but even to those who don't: the sun shines, the rain falls, and the earth produces food for everyone alike. He is so good that He gave us salvation even while we were dead in our sin and not deserving to be saved. Our God is a **benevolent** God.

Psalm 107, Matthew 5:45, James 1:17
*see also **Faithful, Gracious, Merciful***

Merciful

When I was lost, out in the cold, You brought me home into your fold.

When God saves us, it is more than Him holding back judgment that we deserve. Out of His compassion for us, He does for us what we cannot do for ourselves: He heals us, He forgives us, and He becomes our friend. Though we may be lost like stray animals, He brings us out of the cold and dark into the warmth of fellowship and communion with Him. Our God is a **merciful** God.

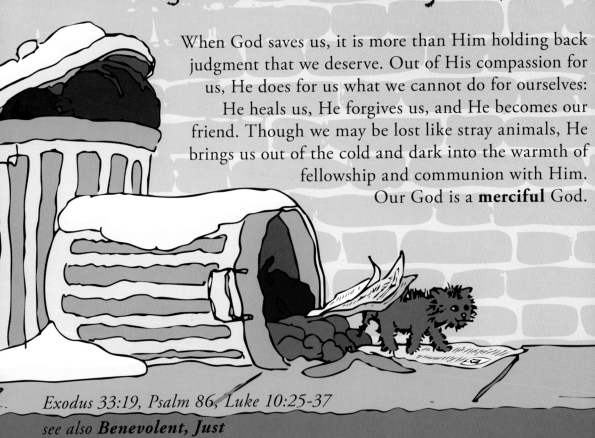

Exodus 33:19, Psalm 86, Luke 10:25-37

see also **Benevolent, Just**

Faithful

God remembers His people:
   His promises are true,
Two thousand years ago,
   today, and tomorrow too.

It is beautiful to see old married couples who have loved each other for a whole lifetime. They are a picture of faithfulness, a friendship that lasts through good times and bad. We may think that the Bible was written to tell us how to be faithful to God. But really, the main story is how God is **faithful** to us. The God that made promises of blessing to Noah, Abraham, Moses, and David is the same God that sent His Son to fulfill that blessing, and the same God who offers a new life to you today. Our God is a faithful God.

Exodus 34:6, Deuteronomy 7:7-10, Psalm 89:1-8
see also **Nurturing, Personal**

Do you have a favorite toy that you could not bear to lose? Perhaps it is an old doll that your parents gave you a long time ago, or a stuffed animal that sleeps in your bed every night. The achy feeling in your heart when your special toy goes missing, the fretful knots in your stomach as you madly go searching for it, and the warm flood of joy that comes with a happy reunion all show your love for it.

There are many signs of God's **love** for us, but none is greater than the search He is on to bring His lost children back home. God sends His Son to look for us, and when we are found, there are great parties in heaven!

Though we may wander
to some place afar,
Our God lovingly calls us,
wherever we are.

Exodus 34:6, Deuteronomy 7:7-13
Psalm 136, Luke 15:8-10, 1 John 4:16
*See also **Benevolent, Faithful, Merciful***

Forgiving

We are given a whole new life,
When God takes away
    our sin and strife.

Imagine that you were to never take a bath or shower, wash your clothes or change into new ones ever again. You would start smelling: first like dirt, then like sweat, then like garbage. Soon no one would want to sit near you because you smelled so bad.

As sin piles on top of sin, we become spiritually dirty and offensive to God. Our stink becomes worse and worse, ultimately leading to spiritual death. Thankfully God is **forgiving**, willing to befriend those who are truly sorry. Yet, God does not merely hold His breath and ignore our stink. Like clean water that washes dirt away, God forgives our wickedness by carrying it away with the sinless blood of Jesus.

Exodus 34:5-7, Psalm 78:38,
Daniel 9:4-19, Ephesians 4:32
*See also **Just, Lamb, Merciful***

One

Not ten, not twenty, not many, not none, The God we worship is the only One.

God is unique; there is no other being like Him in the universe. He is the same God whether you pray to Him from the North Pole or from the South. He is also the same God who talked to Adam, Abraham, Moses, and David, Isaiah, Jeremiah, and Daniel. He is the same God who came into the world as Jesus Christ, and the same God whose Spirit dwells in the people of the church today. Not many, not none, but **one** God!

Deuteronomy 6:4, Isaiah 43:10,
Mark 12:28-30, Romans 3:29-30
see also **Aseity, YHWH**

Just

Sin will try in darkness to stay,
But God brings all secrets to the light of day.

Many people believe that they can get away with evil in this life, because they think that they can hide, or that no one is watching. However, our God is a **just** God, and all evil will be discovered and punished, sooner or later. The gaze of God is like a great spotlight that exposes all the thoughts and actions of everyone. In the end, He will make everything right: He will reveal every secret thing, whether good or bad, and deliver the penalty or reward we deserve.

Thankfully, our God is also a merciful God, and has offered His Son to take that penalty for us so that we can return to friendship with Him. This would be a little bit like you paying your parents for the cookies so that you could share them with the racoon.

Deuteronomy 32:4, Isaiah 42:1-4,
Matthew 6:3-4, John 3:20, Romans 14:10-12
*see also **Benevolent, Merciful***

King

Oh holy King,
    strong and true,
All the world's nations
    belong to you.

2 Samuel 7:13, Revelation 4, 21:24
*see also **Just, Victorious***

There are many countries in the world with different kinds of rulers, but God is **King** over all of them because He made everybody and everything. Though not everyone recognizes God as King today, the Bible tells us that one day, all the nations will bow low, lay down their power and worship Him together.

Judge

Though we may question God's mysterious ways,
He will examine us, at the end of our days.

As we grow older, we may ask God some difficult questions, because life can be full of hard times: "Why do bad things happen to good people?" "Why can't I see you?" "Why don't you give me what I ask for sometimes?" We may even feel like bringing God into a courtroom. But as we have these thoughts, we must always remember that in the end it is God who will **judge** humankind with the questions "Do you really know me?" and "What did you do with the life that I gave you?"

Job 38, Matthew 7:21-23, Mark 11:27-33, Revelation 20:11-15
*see also **Creator, Just, King***

GOD c/o DAVID
7 PALACE WAY
JERUSALEM
JUDAH

GOD c/o PAUL
3 MISSIONARY ROAD
CORINTH
ACHAIA

SPQR

GOD c/o MOSES
40 MOUNTAIN PATH
WADI FEIRAN
SINAI

ALL PEOPLE
EVERY NATION
ENDS-OF-THE-EARTH

Revelation

God did not ignore us
or leave us alone:
He gave us love letters,
so His will would be known.

Have you ever tried to read a letter inside a sealed envelope? Unless you have x-ray vision, it's impossible! You will not know what a letter says until you take it out of the envelope and reveal its contents. A revelation is something that used to be secret, but then has been "opened" so that you now know about it. God has given us many such revelations: the Bible is a collection of these messages, delivered to us through prophets, poets, wise people and apostles. Creation is also like a letter that tells us about the glory of God. Most importantly, Jesus' life on earth was the greatest **revelation** of all.

Psalm 19, John 1:14, 2 Timothy 3:16
see also **Gracious, Word**

Eternal

God's thoughts are deeper than the deepest well, His mind more complex than words can ever tell.

When we stand on the seashore, we feel really tiny because the ocean holds so many things that we cannot see: the countless number of fish and whales swimming through it, the forests of sea plants within it, the continents of people beyond it. We feel small standing next to something that seems to go on forever; this feeling is a small taste of the eternal. Just as our mouths and stomachs could never drink dry the ocean, our minds can never fully understand our **eternal** God.

Psalm 90, 1 Timothy 1:16, Revelation 22:13
*see also **Aseity, Holy***

Incarnate

Though God is big,
    He became a baby, small;
He did this so
    He could be friends with us all.

Even though God is totally different from us, He wants to be with us. And because we could not go to Him, He came to us. Imagine that an elephant wanted to become friends with ants and shrunk himself so that the ants could see him. When Jesus came to earth He became like us by giving up His godly glory. He took on a human body (**incarnate** means "in the flesh") so that He could walk with us and teach us about the invisible things of God.

Isaiah 7:14, Philippians 2:5-11
*see also **Aseity, Understanding***

Anointed

When God had a special job to be done, He sent His Son Jesus, the Chosen One.

When you anoint something, you cover it with oil and rub it in. For example, before you use a new baseball glove in a game, you prepare it by smearing oil over the leather so that the glove can be more flexible and fit your hand.

You may think that 'Christ' is Jesus' last name, but in fact, it means '**Anointed One**'! When a Jewish king or a priest was appointed by God, that person would be anointed with oil, like the way other countries crown their king. The oil was a sign of being God's chosen one. And just as oil prepares the glove for baseball, anointing prepares the person for a new job. Jesus was chosen by God not to win a mere baseball game however, but to save humankind from sin and rule over all creation in victory.

Psalm 89:19-29, Isaiah 61:1-3, Mark 14:1-9
*see also **Incarnate, King, Lamb, Word***

Understanding

When I laugh with joy,
    or whimper in fear,
When I cry out loud,
    I know that You hear.

Our God is not a far away God, like a mad scientist who invented the world and stepped back to watch it like a funny experiment. He is a God who is near us, **understanding** us like a father or a mother; He is in touch with the world, sending His own Son into it to become friends with people. Jesus walked amongst us, empathized with us, and died for us. God understands us not only as an all-powerful being who knows everything, but as a human who knows of all our weaknesses and trials first-hand.

Isaiah 52:13-53:12, Philippians 2:1-11, Hebrews 4:15
see also **Incarnate, Personal**

Lamb

**God saved the sinful human race,
When He punished the spotless Lamb
in our place.**

Aren't baby sheep the cutest creatures on earth? Cuddly,
innocent, and trusting, people naturally love little
lambs. So why would the Bible say that Jesus is the
Lamb of God, and that He needs to be killed?

The reason is that someone must take the punishment
for our sins, someone who is even more innocent and
perfect than a little lamb. This sounds horrible, because
it *is* horrible: our sin is so bad that it can only be erased by
death. Thankfully, after Jesus died for our sin, God raised
him back to life to be honored and praised by all.

Isaiah 53:7, John 1:29, Revelation 5:6
see also **Deliverer, Merciful**

Trinity

Our Heavenly Father,
  Messiah who came,
    Spirit within us,
      You're One and the same.

One of the most mysterious things that God has revealed is the way He works in three persons. The Bible clearly shows our One God connecting with us as the Father, the Son, and the Holy Spirit. The Father directs the universe, the Son suffered for us on the cross, and the Spirit dwells within His people, and yet they are all acting together as well. Each person is fully God, and not just "part" of Him, and yet each person has their distinct roles as well. Even the wisest people have a hard time imagining this strange truth, but the **Trinity** is one of the most beautiful aspects of our God, revealing the importance of communion even within God Himself.

Matthew 28:19-20, John 20:21-22, 2 Corinthians 13:14
see also **One, YHWH, Anointed, Spirit**

Victorious

When we think
the battle's just begun,
The cross tells us
He's already won!

1 Corinthians 15:50-57, Revelation 17:14
see also **Just, King**

Though there are ongoing spiritual battles between the world and God, between demons and angels, and between the doers of wrong and the upholders of right, the war has already been decided. Jesus' death and resurrection at the cross gave Him the complete **victory** over sin and over Satan. As we face our own spiritual struggles today, it should always be with the certain hope of this victory. Like foot soldiers on the front lines knowing that the cavalry is on the way, we can press on knowing that our triumph is guaranteed.

The Beginning and The End

God invites us to be with Him,
    An offer that is free,
To enjoy His holy presence
    For all eternity.

God is **the beginning**: He existed before the formation of the world, and is the creator of everything in the universe. God is also **the end**: the history of *this* world will conclude when Christ finally returns to judge and reward, ushering in the *new* heaven and earth. Like a marriage feast that marks the creation of a new home, there will be a brilliant and glorious banquet for all of God's people, celebrating the new home that we will have in His presence forever and ever, Amen.

Isaiah 60-62, Revelation 21 & 22
*see also **Creator, Personal, Love***

Christian Focus Publications publishes books for adults and children under its four main imprints: Christian Focus, Christian Heritage, CF4K and Mentor. Our books reflect that God's word is reliable and Jesus is the way to know Him, and live for ever with Him.

Our children's publication list includes a Sunday school curriculum that covers pre-school to early teens; puzzle and activity books. We also publish personal and family devotional titles, biographies and inspirational stories that children will love.

If you are looking for quality Bible teaching for children then we have an excellent range of Bible story and age specific theological books.

From pre-school to teenage fiction, we have it covered!

Find us at our web page: *www.christianfocus.com*